HOW I GET AROUND

BUSES

RYAN EARLEY

TABLE OF CONTENTS

Sight Words.................................2

Words to Know.............................3

Index..16

A Pelican Book

SEAHORSE PUBLISHING

Teaching Tips for Caregivers and Teachers:

Research shows that one of the best ways for students to learn a new topic is to read about it.

Before Reading

- Read the title and predict what the book will be about.
- Read the "Words to Know" and discuss the meaning of each word.
- Read the back cover to see what the book is about.

During Reading

- When a student gets to a word that is unknown, ask them to look at the rest of the sentence to find clues to help with the meaning of the unknown word.
- Motivate students with praise and encouragement.

After Reading

- Discuss the main idea of the book.
- Ask students to give one detail that they learned in the book.

Sight Words

all	by	have
are	four	I
around	get	most
big	go	on

Words to Know

bus

lights

roads

wheels

windows

I get around by **bus**.

bus

All buses are big.

Stagecoach
LT385
xford Circus 55
Love Mondays
Get the app and find a job you adore
Reed.co.uk
108
LTZ 1385

Most buses have four big **wheels**.

wheel

lights

All buses have **lights**.

All buses have **windows.**

window

All buses go on **roads**.

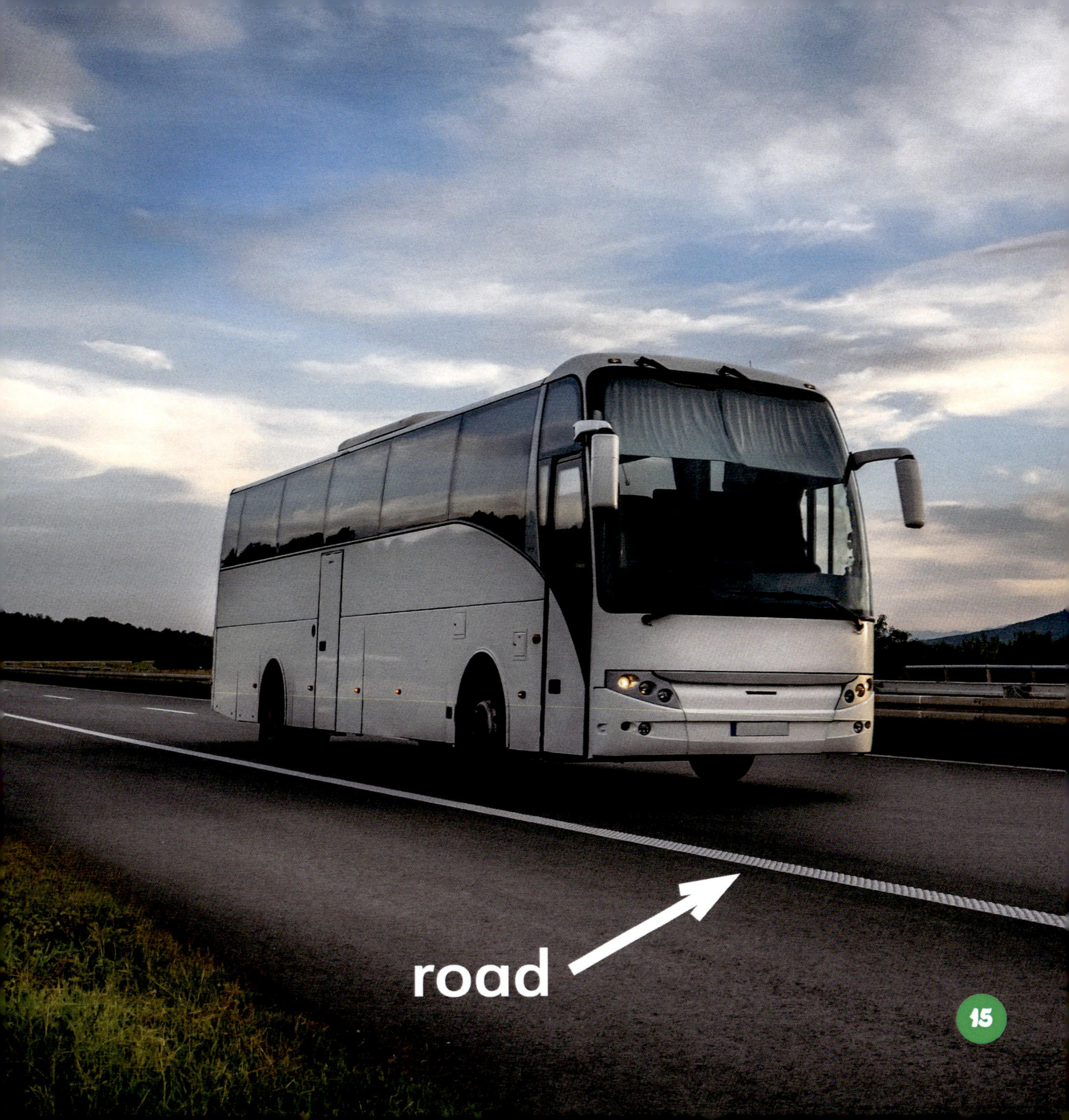
road

Index

big 6–8
lights 10, 11
roads 14, 15
wheels 8, 9
windows 12, 13

Written by: Ryan Earley
Design by: Niko Magaro
Editor: Kim Thompson
Series Development: James Earley

Photos: All images from Shutterstock

Library of Congress PCN Data
Buses / Ryan Earley
How I Get Around
ISBN 979-8-8945-9258-9(hard cover)
ISBN 979-8-8945-9272-5(paperback)
ISBN 979-8-8945-9300-5(EPUB)
ISBN 979-8-8945-9286-2(eBook)
ISBN 979-8-8945-9314-2(audio)
ISBN 979-8-8945-9328-9(Read-Along)
Library of Congress Control Number: 2024946361

Printed in Canada/012025/CP20250101

Seahorse Publishing Company
seahorsepub.com

Published in the United States
Seahorse Publishing
PO Box 771325
Coral Springs, FL 33077

SEAHORSE PUBLISHING